GREAT TEAMS IN HOCKEY HISTORY

Luke DeCock

Raintree

Chicago, Illinois

For more information address the publisher:
Raintree, 100 N. LaSalle, Suite 1200, Chicago IL 60602

Printed and bound in China by WKT Company Limited

10 09 08
10 9 8 7 6 5 4 3 2

Library of Congress Cataloging-in-Publication Data:

DeCock, Luke.
  Great teams in hockey history / Luke DeCock.
      p. cm. — (Great teams)
  Includes bibliographical references and index.
  ISBN 1-4109-1486-0 (hc) — ISBN 1-4109-1493-3 (pb)
  ISBN 978-1-4109-1486-6 (Hc) — ISBN 978-1-4109-1493-4 (Pbk)
  1. National Hockey League—History—20th century—Juvenile literature.
  2. Hockey teams—History—20th century—Juvenile literature. I. Title. II. Series

GV847.8.N3D43 2006
796.962'64—dc22

                                              2005011966

Acknowledgements
The publishers would like to thank the following for permission to reproduce photographs:
Corbis pp. 7 (Bettmann), 10 (Bettmann), 13 (Bettmann), 16 (Bettmann), 25 (Bettmann), 27 (Bettmann), 29 (Bettmann), 31 (Bettmann), 43 (Reuters/Gary C. Caskey), 44 (Reuters/ Pierre DuCharme); Empics pp. 6 (AP Photo), 19 (AP Photo), 20 (AP Photo), 33 (AP), 37 (AP Photo/James A. Finley), 42 (SportsChrome/Rob Tringali Jr.); Getty Images pp. 4 (B. Bennett), 5 (Elsa), 9 (B. Bennett), 11 (B. Bennett), 14 (Hulton Archive), 15 (Hulton Archive), 18 (Melchior DiGiacomo), 21 (B. Bennett), 22 (B. Bennett), 24 , 28 , 32, 34 (B. Bennett), 36 (Focus On Sport), 39 (Robert Laberge), 40 (Brian Bahr), 45 (Rick Stewart).

Cover image reproduced with permission of Getty (NHLI).

Every effort has been made to contact the copyright holders of any material reproduced in this book. Any omissions will be rectified in subsequent printings if notice is given to the publishers.

The paper used to print this book comes from sustainable resources.

Contents

Welcome to the Game 4

1954–1955 Detroit Red Wings 6

1955–1956 Montreal Canadiens 10

1966–1967 Toronto Maple Leafs 14

1969–1970 Boston Bruins 16

1976–1977 Montreal Canadiens 20

1981–1982 New York Islanders 24

1983–1984 Edmonton Oilers 28

1991–1992 Pittsburgh Penguins 32

1993–1994 New York Rangers 36

2000–2001 Colorado Avalanche 40

The Final Score 44

Stanley Cup Winners 1960–2004 45

Glossary 46

Further Information 47

Index 48

Any words appearing in the text in bold, **like this**, are explained in the glossary.

Welcome to the Game

From its origins on the frozen ponds of Canada, to the crowded arenas of today, the game of hockey has always had many loyal fans that cheer every goal, **assist**, and crunching **body check**. But as much as fans enjoy the excitement of watching a game, they also enjoy being part of a game that has almost a century of history.

For many years, there were only six teams in the **National Hockey League (NHL)**. These teams are known as the "Original Six." It was a slower and rougher game then, but it was full of stories. Teams traveled by train, and players had nicknames such as "Punch," "Turk," "Boom-Boom," and "Rocket." Back in the beginning of hockey, players didn't wear the same safety gear that they wear today. Goalies didn't wear masks, players didn't wear helmets or anything to protect their faces, and there were no big shoulder pads like there are today. Just imagine playing hockey with a speeding puck flying at you with no safety equipment!

Today, there are 30 teams in the NHL and hockey's **dynasties** are some of the greatest in sports. Gordie Howe, Wayne Gretzky, Mario Lemieux, and Bobby Orr, the four greatest players in hockey history, all played on championship teams. Hockey is now popular from coast to coast and all the way from Canada to the South. Players wear the best in protective gear, from helmets to goalie masks and thick shoulder pads.

Ted Lindsay of the Detroit Red Wings kisses the Stanley Cup after winning in 1954.

Fans now pack huge arenas every year to cheer for their favorite team. Teams hope that they will get to the **Stanley Cup** finals and win the championship title. Since it takes sixteen wins to capture the Stanley Cup, this makes it the hardest championship in professional sports today.

This book picks ten of the greatest professional hockey teams of all time. It is a difficult choice, because hockey has had an exciting history and many great teams. Many teams had excellent individual players who played well together. Some had players who led the league in goals and assists. Others had great defenses that made it very difficult for their opponents to get near the goal. Many had great goalies that stood like brick walls in front of their goals. Still more had determined coaches that got their players to believe in themselves and come together to play good hockey. All of these teams won the Stanley Cup, and all will be remembered for years to come. After you read this book, you can decide: which is the greatest team in hockey history?

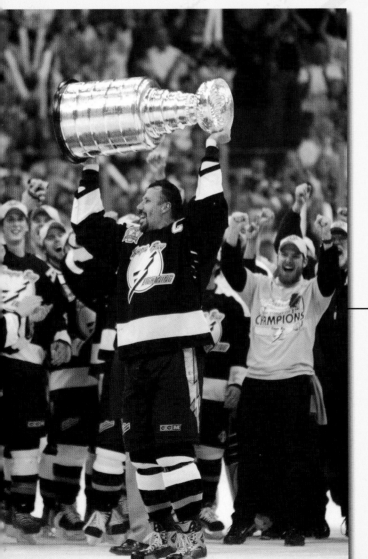

Tampa Bay Lightning players celebrate their victory after defeating the Calgary Flames in the 2004 Stanley Cup Finals.

1954–1955 Detroit Red Wings

Gordie Howe earned the nickname "Mr. Hockey" by playing in more games than anyone else and setting scoring records that weren't broken until the 1980s. He played hockey throughout five **decades**, and enjoyed individual success throughout his years as a player. Howe won four Stanley Cups with the Red Wings in the early 1950s. The Detroit Red Wings finished first in the league seven straight times from 1948–1949 through 1954–1955.

The Red Wings were a great team, and Howe had some help in 1954–1955. The Red Wings had the best offensive attack in hockey with the high-scoring, hard-hitting "Production Line" of Howe, "Terrible" Ted Lindsay, and Alex Delvecchio. In 1952–1953, Howe led the league with 95 points and Lindsay was second with 71 as the Red Wings scored 222 goals. None of the other five teams in the NHL scored more than 169 goals.

Detroit goalie Terry Sawchuck is lifted into the air after he helped his team win the NHL championship game against the Montreal Canadiens.

In 1952, two brothers, Jerry and Pete Cusimano, thought that it would be good luck to throw an octopus on the ice. The brothers thought that each arm of the octopus could represent one of the wins needed for the Stanley Cup. When the Red Wings swept through the playoffs that year, the octopus became a lasting part of hockey, and Detroit became the best team in the league.

The Motor City Work Ethic

"The Production Line" was a good nickname for the Red Wings' top **forward line** of Gordie Howe, Ted Lindsay, and Alex Delvecchio. Not only could that line score lots of goals, they also represented the spirit of the city. In the years after World War II, there was a huge growth of the auto industry in Detroit, Michigan. Many fans worked on the production line in an auto plant, such as Ford's massive River Rouge complex, and then relaxed by watching the Red Wings play. In a hard-working city, the Red Wings were especially appreciated because they tried hard in every game.

After their seventh straight first-place finish, the Red Wings faced the Toronto Maple Leafs in the first round of the playoffs. They easily beat Toronto in four games, moving on to the Stanley Cup finals where they faced the Montreal Canadiens. The Canadiens had reached the finals for their fifth straight year. The two teams had met earlier in the regular season, when both teams were tied for first place. Montreal's fans had gotten out of control and started a riot.

Inside the arena, the fans threw food, programs, and a tear gas bomb. Outside, they ran wild in the streets, smashing windows and breaking into stores and cars. Because of the riot, tensions between the teams and their fans were very high. It would be an interesting match-up.

Ted Lindsay scored many goals for the Red Wings.

1954–1955 Detroit Red Wings

In Game 1 of the Stanley Cup finals, Detroit's Marty Pavelich and Ted Lindsay scored goals late in the game to lead the Red Wings to a 4–2 victory. Lindsay continued his great playing in Game 2, scoring an amazing 4 goals to lead the Red Wings to an easy 7–1 victory. Marcel Pronovost, Howe, and Delvecchio also scored for Detroit. Detroit now led the series, two games to none. However, Montreal didn't give up. They came back in Game 3 and won behind Bernie "Boom-Boom" Geoffrion's 2 goals. Montreal then used the **momentum** from their Game 3 win and won Game 4 against Detroit, 5–3. Earl "Dutch" Reibel tried to keep the Red Wings in the game by scoring two goals, but it just wasn't enough.

The series was now tied 2–2. Playing great like he had been all season, Howe scored a **hat trick** (3 goals) for his team, and they cruised to a 5–1 victory in Game 5. All Detroit needed was one more victory to win the Stanley Cup, but Montreal wasn't ready to give up. In Game 6, the Canadiens showed they wanted to be champions just as much as the Red Wings did. They won 6–3. The series was now tied 3–3, and the final Game 7 would determine which team would be crowned champions. People started to call the series a "homer's series," because every victory in the series was won at the home team's arena.

Game 7 was intense. It was at the Red Wings' arena and the team hadn't lost a home game in four months. The "Production Line" carried them through. They weren't going to let the Canadiens beat them at home, and won an exciting 3–1 game to clinch the Stanley Cup. Delvecchio was the offensive star of the game, scoring 2 goals, while Howe added 1, his ninth goal of the playoffs. Howe set a playoffs record with 20 points in 11 games. The victory gave Detroit's general manager, Jack Adams, his seventh Stanley Cup!

1954–1955 Record

Won	Lost	Tied	Playoffs
42	17	11	Defeated Toronto Maple Leafs 4–0
			Defeated Montreal Canadiens 4–3

Gordie Howe (1928–   )

With his long history in the game, and his talented playing ability, Gordie Howe earned the nickname "Mr. Hockey." He was among the NHL's top five scorers for twenty straight seasons. He led the league in scoring six times and was named **Most Valuable Player (MVP)** six times. In the process, Howe set records for games played, points, goals, and assists. It wasn't until Wayne Gretzky came along that Howe's records were broken. The two played together in the **World Hockey Association (WHA)**. In 1979–1980, when that league merged with the NHL, Gretzky's first NHL season was Howe's last. In 1997, Howe actually played with the minor-league Detroit Vipers to make it five decades of playing pro hockey.

The 1950s saw Montreal **dominate** the NHL like no team had ever done before. Maurice Richard was a hero to people who spoke both French and English, and he became the first player to score 50 goals. Forwards such as "Boom-Boom" Geoffrion, who invented the slapshot, and Jean Beliveau, who led the league in scoring, became fan favorites. With Doug Harvey on defense and Jacques Plante in goal, the Canadiens won five straight Stanley Cups.

While the 1955–1956 team was the best of those five, a year earlier the Canadiens had been in trouble. Fans rioted during a game against the Detroit Red Wings because Richard had been suspended for the 1955 playoffs, after he hit a player with his stick. Montreal missed Richard and ended up losing to the Red Wings in the finals. The next year, with Richard on the team, Montreal was unstoppable.

The Canadiens were a great team that featured twelve future **Hockey Hall of Fame** players, including manager Frank Selke and coach Toe Blake. During the regular season, Beliveau won the scoring title with 47 goals, earning the **Art Ross Trophy** for leading goalscorer. He also set a record for most goals and assists as a center. Bert Olmstead, the team's left wing, also set a record with 56 assists.

Toe Blake coached the Canadiens during the 1955-1956 season.

Jean Beliveau (1931–   )

Jean Beliveau was among the league's leading scorers for two decades and was team captain during some of the Canadiens' greatest years. He retired after the Canadiens won the Cup in 1971, and he became the first player to skate a lap of the ice with the trophy. After his retirement, Beliveau was often urged to run for political office. In 1994, he was asked to become Governor General of Canada, which was a great honor. Beliveau said no, out of modesty. In 2003, when Montreal fans booed the United States' anthem in protest of the war in Iraq, the team played a videotaped message from Beliveau. No one booed after that.

The Canadiens were so talented on the **power play** that they forced a rule change. Previously, players would serve the full two minutes of their penalty. Montreal scored so often, this rule was changed to end the penalty after a goal was scored against the other team. Richard was at his best, scoring 38 goals. The Canadiens had a fantastic goalie in Jacques "Jake the Snake" Plante. He was the first modern goaltender. He left the net to play the puck and charge shooters instead of waiting for them to shoot. Plante won five straight **Vezina Trophies** as the best goalie in the league and had two **shutouts** in the 1956 playoffs.

Montreal ended the regular season with a 24-point lead over their nearest opponent, the second-placed Red Wings. In the semi-finals of the playoffs, the Canadiens faced the New York Rangers. They won the series four games to one, and advanced to the Stanley Cup finals for the second straight year. In the other semi-final series, Detroit beat Toronto four games to one, setting up a rematch of the previous year's finals.

In Game 1 of the finals, the Red Wings played better for the first two **periods**. Montreal came back in the third period behind goals from Beliveau, Geoffrion, and Claude Provost and ended up winning 6–4. The Canadiens continued to score a lot of goals in Game 2 and beat Detroit 5–1. Detroit, the defending champions, would not be pushed around though. In Game 3, behind goals from Kelly, Lindsay, and Howe, the Red Wings won 3–1, bringing the series to 2–1.

HISTORY BOX

Carrying the Flag

English-speaking colonists and immigrants settled most of Canada, but the French settled the area that is now Quebec. Quebec is very proud of its language and traditions, and the Canadiens are extremely popular there. The team is fondly known as "The Habs," short for "Les Habitants." This is a French term meaning "the country boys" or "the local boys." Local players such as Maurice "Rocket" Richard, Jean Beliveau, and Guy Lafleur are heroes to this day.

1955–1956 Record

Won	Lost	Tied	Playoffs
45	15	10	Defeated New York Rangers 4–1
			Defeated Detroit Red Wings 4–1

The defense of the Canadiens was outstanding in Game 4. Beliveau scored 2 goals and Floyd Curry added 1 to lead their team to a 3–0 victory. Montreal was now up three games to one, and was only one victory away from the Stanley Cup. They wanted the championship badly and won the next game 4–1 to take the Cup. Beliveau and Geoffrion continued their great offensive play, each scoring a goal in the game. In the playoffs, Beliveau scored an amazing twelve goals, two being game winners, and had seven assists. He finished the season with a total of 59 goals. The Canadiens were not finished there. They went on to win the Stanley Cup for the next four seasons, stretching out their championship run to five years!

The Montreal Canadiens' coach is hoisted into the air to celebrate their victory over the Red Wings.

Few teams are remembered as fondly in their home city as the 1966–1967 Toronto Maple Leafs. It was the last season for many of the team's popular players who were getting ready to retire. The goalies were 42-year-old Johnny Bower and 37-year-old Terry Sawchuck. Three key players—Red Kelly, Bob Pulford, and George "Chief" Armstrong—were all 39. Coach Punch Imlach had to take time off to rest during the season. However, the Maple Leafs finished third and faced the league's best team, the Chicago Blackhawks, in the semi-finals. Bower was injured during Game 5 and Terry Sawchuck took his place. Sawchuck had 49 saves in 40 minutes as the Maple Leafs won and moved on to the finals against the Montreal Canadiens.

Two Canadian teams would battle for the championship. The Maple Leafs and Canadiens had been the champions in 18 of the past 24 seasons, so it was no surprise to see them facing each other. The Canadiens entered the final series on a fifteen-game unbeaten streak. In Game 1, Terry Sawchuck started in goal for the Maple Leafs and couldn't stop the Canadiens as they scored 4 goals against him. The Canadiens rolled to a 6–2 victory. Coach Imlach wasn't pleased with Sawchuck's performance and started Bower in goal for Game 2. It was a good decision. Bower stopped all 31 shots he faced and the Maple Leafs won 3–0 behind goals from Pete Stemkowski, Mike Walton, and Tim Horton. The series was tied at 1–1.

Dave Keon attacks the goal during the 1967 Stanley Cup finals.

1966–1967 Record

Won	Lost	Tied	Playoffs
32	27	11	Defeated Chicago Blackhawks 4–2
			Defeated Montreal Canadiens 4–2

Terry Sawchuck watches as the Canadiens threaten to score in Game 1 of the Stanley Cup.

Game 3 was a great defensive game by both goalies. Bower faced 63 shots on goal and gave up only 2. The game stretched into **overtime**, and then it went into double overtime. Toronto's Bob Pulford scored the game-winning goal. Before Game 4, Bower hurt his leg and the Maple Leafs were forced to start Sawchuck, who once again could not stop the Canadiens. He allowed 6 goals, which gave Montreal a 6–2 victory. The series was tied again, at 2–2.

Surprisingly, Sawchuck started Game 5. This time, however, he was ready to play. The first two periods of the game he dove all over the ice, stopping every shot that came near him. Toronto scored three goals in the second period and broke the game open. In the third period, Toronto's defense was great, as they made it hard for the Canadiens to shoot and pass near their goal. They held on to win 4–1, coming within 1 win of the Stanley Cup.

Coach Imlach stuck with Sawchuck for Game 6, and the goalie stopped all 17 first period shots against him. Ron Ellis and Jim Pappin scored in the second period, giving the Maple Leafs a 2–0 lead. The Canadiens came back and scored a goal, making it 2–1. In the final minute, with the Canadiens threatening to score, a **face-off** was called in Toronto's zone. Coach Imlach made a daring move and sent in an all-**veteran** lineup. Once again, his coaching proved to be great and Allan Stanley, age 41, won the face-off against Montreal's star Jean Beliveau. George Armstrong broke away for a goal and the Leafs clinched a 3–1 victory. This made them champions for the fourth time in six years. It was their thirteenth Stanley Cup.

1969–1970 Boston Bruins

One of hockey's greatest pictures is of Boston Bruins' defenseman Bobby Orr diving through the air after scoring to win the 1970 Stanley Cup. Orr was a very talented player. His greatest moment was scoring the game-winning goal for the Cup, and the 1969–1970 Boston Bruins was the best team he played on.

The Bruins won the Cup in 1970 and 1972, partly because they traded for a high-scoring center named Phil Esposito in 1967. Esposito was 25 years old and scored 21 goals and 40 assists to finish seventh in the NHL that season. The following season, in 1968–1969, Esposito continued his great offensive play. That season, he became the first player in the league to score over 100 points. Once he got to Boston, Esposito finished either first or second in scoring in each of the next eight seasons. Behind Esposito and Orr, the Bruins were an unstoppable team.

Bobby Orr and Phil Esposito recieve their awards for their achievements in the 1969-1970 season.

On the defensive end, the Bruins were very tough. The goalie, Gerry Cheevers, was a colorful character. He painted stitches on his goalie mask to show where pucks had hit him. Orr's defensive play was also changing the game of hockey. Before Orr, defensemen didn't try to score. But Orr liked to skate with the puck and pass. He set up goals like no one else before him. Orr showed that defensemen could do more than just defend. He was the first, and only, defenseman to win a scoring title with 120 points in 1969–1970. That year, Orr also set an NHL record for 87 assists. He could score, pass, and defend, and this made him one of the game's great players.

During the regular season the Bruins played in the Eastern division, which was a very close division. Only seven points separated the first through fifth place teams. Meanwhile, the Western division was very different. The St. Louis Blues won, winning their division by eighteen points.

HISTORY BOX

Growing the Game

The Bruins rose to the top of the NHL at an exciting time for the league. For 24 years, the league had consisted of 6 teams that had been around since 1926. But for the 1967–1968 season, the NHL expanded to Philadelphia, Los Angeles, St. Louis, Minnesota, Pittsburgh, and Oakland. Other professional sports had added teams before. For hockey, this addition was the first step in becoming a major sport. By 2000, the league had grown from 6 to 30 teams.

1969–1970 Boston Bruins

The Blues and the Bruins met in the Stanley Cup finals. In the first game the Bruins came out strong, scoring an amazing 4 goals in the third period for an easy 6–1 victory over St. Louis. John Bucyk led Boston and he scored a hat trick for his team, with a goal coming in each period. In Game 2, Boston once again showed they were the better team, by scoring 6 goals. They won the game 6–2.

In Game 3, St. Louis showed they weren't going to back down as they took an early lead. The Bruins fought back behind goals from Bucyk and John McKenzie, and the team took a small 2–1 lead in the third period. In the last period, it was Boston's game, as Wayne Cashman scored 2 goals to give the Bruins a 4–1 victory and a 3–0 series lead. They were now only one game away from a **sweep** and the Stanley Cup.

Bobby Orr (1948–   )

Bobby Orr's No. 4 is retired in Boston, but he is honored everywhere hockey is played. With his skating and skills, he created a new role for defensemen. For Orr, scoring goals was as important as stopping the other team from scoring them. He won three straight Hart Trophies as the league's Most Valuable Player and eight straight Norris Trophies as its best defenseman. A bad left knee forced him to retire in 1978 after only eight seasons. Orr remains one of the game's great players.

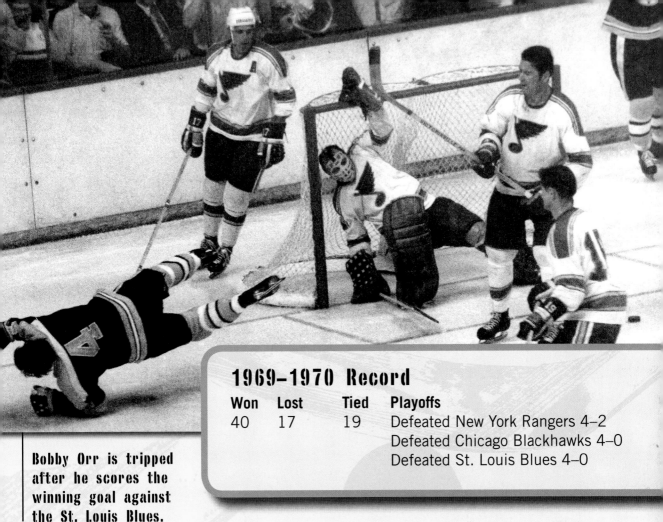

Bobby Orr is tripped after he scores the winning goal against the St. Louis Blues.

1969–1970 Record

Won	Lost	Tied	Playoffs
40	17	19	Defeated New York Rangers 4–2
			Defeated Chicago Blackhawks 4–0
			Defeated St. Louis Blues 4–0

St. Louis played very tough in Game 4, with a rough defense and hard-hitting body checks to the Bruins players. It was Boston, however, who scored first. St. Louis came back and scored 2 quick goals to take a 2–1 lead. Boston's regular season star, Esposito, tied the game at 2–2. The Blues' Larry Keenan scored early in the last period to give the Blues a slim 3–2 lead. With 6 minutes left, Boston scored again, tying the game at 3–3. The game was forced into overtime.

Orr's greatest moment came in overtime. Orr flipped the puck into the goal for the game winner. Right after he scored, Orr was tripped up by Noel Picard. He went flying arms first through the air, completely level with the ice. The photo of that moment is one of the most famous hockey images of all time.

The Stanley Cup victory was one of the great moments in the history of the city of Boston, which had waited 29 years to win the Cup again. They would have to wait only two years for the next, with Orr again scoring the series-winning goal.

1976–1977 Montreal Canadiens

The greatest dynasty the hockey world has known was the Montreal Canadiens of the mid to late 1960s and 1970s. The team truly earned their nickname—Les Glorieux, or The Glorious. The Canadiens won ten Cups in fifteen years.

Montreal player Serge Savard lifts the Stanley Cup above his head to celebrate the championship.

Montreal's best team was the 1976–1977 squad that won the Stanley Cup that season. They won a league high of 60 games and had only 8 losses! The way the Canadiens played changed the game. They scored a lot of goals, but concentrated on defense. The Canadiens had nine future Hall of Famers on the roster: Ken Dryden in goal with Guy Lapointe, Larry Robinson, and Serge Savard on defense. Jacques Lemaire and Bob Gainey were center, and Guy Lafleur, Yvan Cournoyer, and Steve Schutt were on the wings. Sam Pollack was the general manager, and Scotty Bowman was the coach. Both Pollack and Bowman are also in the Hall of Fame.

Lafleur led the league in scoring with 136 points, and Schutt led the league in goals with 60, a record for a left wing. The Canadiens had 132 points in 80 games—a record that hasn't been broken. They lost only once at their home arena, the Forum. This defeat was to the Bruins, early in the year. However, the Canadiens got a chance for revenge in the Stanley Cup finals.

The Canadiens were just as dominant in the first two rounds of the playoffs as they were in the regular season. They swept St. Louis and beat the Islanders to advance to the Cup finals. They met the Boston Bruins in the championship.

Ken Dryden (1947–   )

In 1971, Canadiens' coach Scotty Bowman picked a rookie goalie named Ken Dryden as his playoff starter. Dryden had played in only six NHL games, but the Canadiens won the Cup. Dryden was named Rookie of the Year the next season. Dryden was more than a goalie. He sat out the 1973–1974 season to attend law school. He even wrote a book called *The Game*, which is considered one of the finest books about hockey. Dryden's hockey career was short, but brilliant. In eight seasons, he won the Vezina Trophy as best goalie five times, the **Conn Smythe Trophy** as playoff MVP twice, and played on six Stanley Cup-winning teams.

1976–1977 Montreal Canadiens

The Canadiens showed that they wanted the championship by scoring 2 goals in the first 5 minutes against the Bruins in Game 1. They took only 24 shots all game, but an unbelievable 7 of those shots got past Boston's goalie Gerry Cheevers. The Canadiens dominated and won 7–3. Yvon Lambert and Mario Tremblay each scored two goals for Montreal. As in Game 1, Montreal took very few shots on goal in Game 2. They shot only nineteen times, but three shots were for goals. Steve Shutt was Montreal's offensive hero, scoring a goal and assisting on two. Canadiens goalie Ken Dryden blocked all 21 shots he faced as Montreal shut out the Bruins 3–0. They now held a 2–0 series lead.

Montreal's Guy Lafleur (center, in white) battles for the puck against the Cleveland Barons.

1976–1977 Record

Won	Lost	Tied	Playoffs
60	8	12	Defeated St. Louis Blues 4–0
			Defeated New York Islanders 4–2
			Defeated Boston Bruins 4–0

HISTORY BOX

Spending Time With the Cup

Guy Lafleur scored many goals in 1976–1977, but one of the biggest in his career came during the 1979 Stanley Cup finals. He scored late in the third period of Game 7 to tie the game. The Canadiens won the game and the Cup in overtime. While his teammates celebrated that night, Lafleur stole the Cup from the trunk of a car. He showed it off on the lawn of his home. He escaped punishment only because of his popularity. Today, every player on the winning team gets to spend a day with the Cup.

In Game 3 the Canadiens continued to dominate. In the first period they took only six shots, but three went in! The Bruins could not stop them and they won 4–2. Facing a sweep in Game 4, the Bruins came out fighting. They got their first lead of the entire series on a goal from Bobby Schmautz, but the Canadiens came right back to tie in the second period. No team scored again, so the game went into overtime. Although it was the best game the Bruins had played all series, they were just no match for Montreal. Four minutes into overtime Lemaire scored, on an assist from Lafleur, for the game and Cup-winning goal. The victory gave the Canadiens their twentieth Stanley Cup. Lafleur, who led the playoffs in scoring with 26 points, received the Conn Smythe Trophy, given to the most outstanding player in the playoffs.

No team that came before dominated the game the way the Canadiens did. They won an amazing twelve of fourteen games in the playoffs. No team that came after had as much pure talent as that team. There would be great players, such as Wayne Gretzky and Mario Lemieux, in the years to come, but no team ever won as easily as the Canadiens did in 1977.

Playing on Long Island in the New York suburbs, the Islanders were a rare team. They were a team without a city. The Islanders' fans considered themselves New Yorkers at heart, but they had to come from all over Long Island to cheer on their team against the New York Rangers.

The Islanders had powerful forwards such as Bryan Trottier, Mike Bossy, and Clark Gillies, and a great defenseman in Denis Potvin. In the net, Billy Smith used his stick to stop pucks and hack at the ankles of any player who got near him.

The Islanders won four straight Stanley Cups between 1979 and 1983.

HISTORY BOX

Rival Leagues Merge

After decades in which there were only six pro hockey teams, the 1970s saw the sport change with the NHL's growth to twenty teams. There was also a new league. The World Hockey Association was founded in 1972 with twelve teams. Bobby Hull was the first NHL star to sign with the rival association for the amazing sum of $1 million! While the NHL had a defensive game, the WHA was all about offense. The WHA collapsed in 1979 and four teams—Edmonton, Hartford, Quebec, and Winnipeg—were invited to join the established league. The Islanders beat Quebec on their way to the Stanley Cup in 1982.

In 1982, the Islanders were at their best, winning their third of four straight Stanley Cups. They led the NHL in wins during the regular season, at one point setting a record with fifteen straight wins. The Islanders went into the playoffs as favorites to win the Cup.

Islanders' player Denis Potvin waits for the puck.

However, the first round didn't go as smoothly as they might have liked. They faced a tough Pittsburgh Penguins team. The Islanders started the series strong, winning the first two games. But then they didn't play as well and lost the next two games. The series was tied at 2–2, and it all came down to Game 5. It was a great game. The Islanders were down 1 goal with only 2:21 remaining when John Tonelli scored a goal and forced overtime. Tonelli continued his heroic play in overtime and scored the game winner, sending his team to the next round.

The Islanders then beat the New York Rangers in six games and swept the Quebec Nordiques to advance to the Stanley Cup finals against the Vancouver Canucks. However, in Game 1, the Canucks played great and led 5–4 with only 7 minutes remaining in the game. Their lead didn't last long against the great Islanders. Mike Bossy scored a goal to tie the game at 5–5 with less than 5 minutes to play. Neither team scored again and the game went into overtime. Both teams played great defense in overtime and it looked as if the game would be sent to double overtime. But with only two seconds left, Bossy scored another goal to steal the win.

Vancouver came out strong again in Game 2, holding onto a slim 3–2 lead going into the final period. New York came back, scoring 2 quick goals to take back the lead, 4–3. The Islanders never looked back, scoring 2 more goals for a 6-4 win and 2–0 series lead.

Mike Bossy (1957–   )

In 1982, Mike Bossy scored one of the most memorable goals in Stanley Cup history. Shoved away from the net by an opposing player, Bossy managed to get his stick on the puck as he fell. With both feet in the air, he fired a backhand into the net. Bossy had a gift for scoring, and it served him well. He is still the only player in NHL history with 9 straight 50-goal seasons. Bossy was important for another reason. He didn't like fighting because other players beat him up when he was young. At the time that Bossy played, fighting was a big part of hockey. Thanks to players like him, the NHL became less violent.

1981–1982 Record

Won	Lost	Tied	Playoffs
54	16	10	Defeated Pittsburgh Penguins 3–2
			Defeated New York Rangers 4–2
			Defeated Quebec Nordiques 4–0
			Defeated Vancouver Canucks 4–0

New York dominated both offensively and defensively in Game 3. They shut out the Canucks, as Clark Gillies, Bob Nystrom, and Mike Bossy all scored goals for a 3–0 victory and 3–0 series lead. The Islanders were only one game away from a sweep and Stanley Cup trophy.

The Canucks didn't want to be swept in the finals, but there wasn't much they could do to stop the Islanders. Mike Bossy proved that he was a great playoff player as he scored two goals in the game. The Canucks never threatened the Islanders as New York won 4–0, earning the Cup and sweeping their opponent. Bossy's seventeen post-season goals led to his winning the Conn Smythe Trophy.

1983–1984 Edmonton Oilers

The greatest player the game of hockey has ever known, Wayne Gretzky, could do anything. He set records for goals, assists, and points in a career and in a single season that may never be broken. He retired with 61 NHL records. He played on many great teams, but the best was the 1983–1984 Edmonton Oilers.

To win his first Stanley Cup, Gretzky had to beat the New York Islanders in 1984. The Islanders had won four Stanley Cups in a row and in 1982–1983, the Islanders had beaten the Oilers for the Cup. Oilers' coach Glen Sather had promised that the next season his team would score 100 points, win the division, and win the Stanley Cup. Sather stuck to his word, as the 1983–1984 Oilers achieved every goal he set for them. Edmonton won the Cup and became hockey's new dynasty. The Oilers won four Cups in five years before Gretzky was traded to the Los Angeles Kings.

With Gretzky in the middle, the Oilers were the best offensive team ever. The 1983–1984 Oilers won 57 games and set a record with 446 goals. Gretzky, Jari Kurri, and Glenn Anderson all scored 50 or more goals for the Oilers. Only the great Mario Lemieux could keep the Oilers from dominating the individual leaders. Twice, the Oilers had 3 players who were 50-goal scorers and 4 players who were 100-point scorers. This had never been done before. Grant Fuhr and Mark Messier were also great players.

Wayne Gretzky lifts the Stanley Cup in 1984.

In the first round of the playoffs, the Oilers faced Winnipeg. The Oilers swept the Jets. In the second round, the Oilers faced a much tougher opponent in the Calgary Flames. The series went all the way to the deciding Game 7, where the Oilers earned the victory to advance to the next round. In the semi-finals, the Oilers faced Minnesota, who they easily swept to earn their spot in the Stanley Cup finals.

It was the second straight year they had reached the finals, where they met the New York Islanders, who had beaten them the previous year and were going for their fifth straight Cup. It would be a great series.

Grant Fuhr (1962–   )

Grant Fuhr had a tough job. The Oilers scored so many goals that they didn't have to play much defense. That left him alone as the goalie. His statistics weren't very good, so sometimes fans ignored him. But he was also a **pioneer**, the game's first great black goalie and one of its first black stars. Ten years after Fuhr played in the NHL, there were more than a dozen African-American goalies playing at the top level in hockey. Fuhr was inducted into the Hockey Hall of Fame in 2003.

Game 1 of the finals was a great defensive match. No team scored in the first two periods as Oilers goalie Grant Fuhr and Islanders goalie Billy Smith played incredible in the net. Someone had to score, and in the third period Oilers Kevin McClelland broke free for a goal. It was all Edmonton needed as they shut out the defending champions 1–0.

New York showed why they had won 4 straight Cups in Game 2 as Clark Gillies scored a hat trick. The Islanders coasted to an easy 6–1 victory, tying the series at 1–1. The teams switched roles in Game 3 as Edmonton did most of the scoring. Edmonton's Glenn Anderson and Paul Coffey scored two goals only seventeen seconds apart. They eventually scored 5 more goals, 3 coming in the last period, for the easy 7–2 victory. Edmonton now led the series 2–1.

Wayne Gretzky scored 2 goals in Game 4 as the Oilers won again, 7–2. Edmonton led the series 3–1 against the defending champions. With a chance for the Oilers to earn the Stanley Cup if they won in Game 5, Gretzky came out playing great. He scored the first two goals of the game, both on assists by Jari Kurri. Gretzky then showed he could pass too, as he assisted Ken Linseman for a goal. Kurri scored one himself and gave the Oilers a strong 4–0 lead. The Islanders tried to come back, but Edmonton was just too strong. The Oilers ended up winning 5–2, clinching the Stanley Cup.

On August 9, 1988, the hockey world was shocked when the Oilers traded Gretzky and two other players to the Kings for two players, three first-round picks, and cash. The Oilers had won four Cups with Gretzky. They won one after he left, but the team was never as good as they were in 1984.

1983–1984 Record

Won	Lost	Tied	Playoffs
57	18	5	Defeated Winnipeg Jets 3–0
			Defeated Calgary Flames 4–3
			Defeated Minnesota North Stars 4–0
			Defeated New York Islanders 4–1

HISTORY BOX

Gretzky Goes West

The trade that sent Wayne Gretzky west to the Los Angeles Kings was very surprising. But it changed hockey forever by making it popular in new places. Hockey had always been popular in Canada. Now people in Hollywood liked it, too. The United States was changing. People were moving from states such as Pennsylvania and Ohio to states such as Arizona and California to find work. Soon, the NHL would put teams in those warm-weather places for the fans that moved there. Because of players like Gretzky, people all over the country wanted to be part of the excitement of pro hockey.

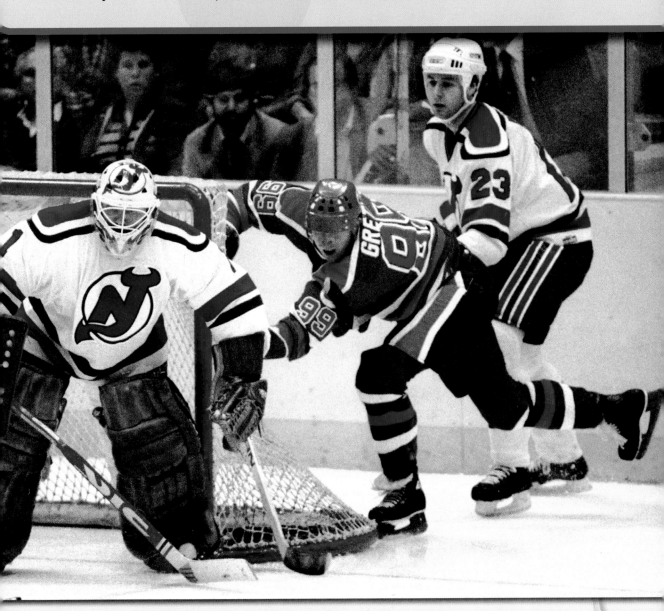

1991–1992 Pittsburgh Penguins

The Penguins were a last-place team when Mario Lemieux arrived in the fall of 1984. But general manager Craig Patrick went about building a team around Lemieux, and by 1992 the Pittsburgh Penguins were the best team in the NHL. With Lemieux leading the way, and stars such as Jaromir Jagr and Ron Francis helping him, the Penguins won back-to-back Cups in 1991 and 1992.

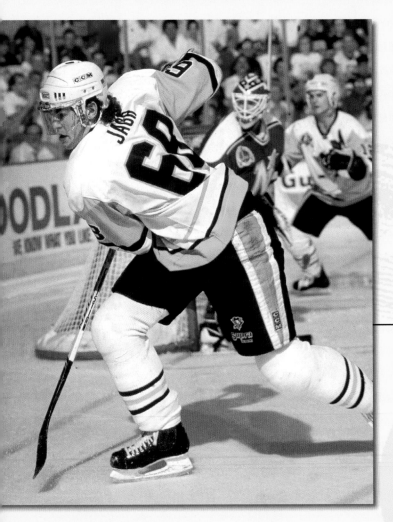

Lemieux was bigger than the great Wayne Gretzky, standing 7 feet tall in skates, but had the same skills and grasp of the game. Only untimely injuries and illness slowed him down. But it took a long time for Lemieux to become a winner. It wasn't until 1991 that the Penguins were good enough to win the Stanley Cup.

Jaromir Jagr helped the Penguins win the Stanley Cup in 1991 and 1992.

While they were celebrating their 1991 Cup, tragedy struck. Coach "Badger" Bob Johnson was diagnosed with a brain tumor and died in November. Rallying around the memory of their lost coach, and behind new coach Scotty Bowman, the Penguins finished third in their division. They were ready for the playoffs and their chance to defend their title.

In the playoffs, Pittsburgh beat the Washington Capitals, New York Rangers, and Boston Bruins to advance to the finals. Pittsburgh met the Chicago Blackhawks in the Stanley Cup finals. The Blackhawks had been unstoppable early in the playoffs, winning eleven straight games. Instead of being worried about how Chicago was playing, the Penguins remembered that they were the defending Cup champions and that they were the best team in the league.

Scotty Bowman took over as coach after the death of Bob Johnson.

HISTORY BOX

Head to Head

There had been other great battles for the scoring title before. Gordie Howe and Maurice Richard spent the 1950s trying to outdo each other. But the hockey world had never seen anything like the scoring race between Mario Lemieux and Wayne Gretzky fought from 1987 to 1994. Before the 1987 season started, Gretzky had led the league for seven straight years. That year, he played in only 64 games and Lemieux scored 70 goals to beat out Gretzky for the title, 168 points to 149. Lemieux won the next year as well, with 199 points to Gretzky's 168, The next two seasons, injuries slowed Lemieux and Gretzky reclaimed the title. Lemieux bounced back to win in 1992–1993 and Gretzky in 1993–1994—his last scoring title. Lemieux won two more, to give him six in his career. Gretzky won ten.

1991–1992 Pittsburgh Penguins

In Game 1 of the finals, Chicago jumped out to a 3–0 lead. Instead of giving up, the Penguins tried to come back. Phil Bourque scored for Pittsburgh to make it a 3–1 game at the end of the opening period. Chicago scored again in the second, making it a 4–1 game. The Penguins' Mario Lemieux and Rick Tocchet scored late in the second period to bring them within one goal at 4–3. With less than five minutes left in the game, Penguins' star Jaromir Jagr scored an unbelievable backhand goal, surrounded by three Blackhawk defenders. The game was tied and looked as if it would be heading into overtime. However, with only thirteen seconds remaining, Lemieux scored a goal to win the game.

Pittsburgh's Bob Errey scored the first goal of Game 2. Chicago came back in the second period and tied. Lemieux, the Penguins' superstar, took over, scoring 2 goals to give his team a 3–1 lead. The Penguins' defense then worked extra hard, only allowing Chicago four shots on goal in the last period. They held for a 3–1 win, taking a 2–0 series lead.

Game 3 was a very good defensive game. Penguins' goalie Tom Barrasso stopped all thirteen Chicago shots in the first period. Kevin Stevens scored the only goal of the game for Pittsburgh, giving them a 1–0 victory. Facing a sweep, Chicago came out strong in Game 4. They led 3–0 early, but in the third period it was tied at 4–4. Pittsburgh's Kevin Stevens and Ron Francis both scored to make it 6–4. Chicago's Jeremy Roenick scored to make it 6–5, but the Blackhawks could not get any closer. Pittsburgh swept the Blackhawks for their second straight Cup. Lemieux was given the Conn Smythe Trophy, his second year in a row.

1991–1992 Record

Won	Lost	Tied	Playoffs
39	32	9	Defeated Washington Capitals 4–3
			Defeated New York Rangers 4–2
			Defeated Boston Bruins 4–0
			Defeated Chicago Blackhawks 4–0

More tragedy would keep the Penguins from gaining a third Cup. Lemieux was diagnosed with cancer in January 1993, and though he beat it and returned to the ice that season, he played only 22 games in the next 2 seasons. Lemieux returned with an excellent individual performance, leading the league in scoring in 1995–1996 and 1996–1997. Sadly, though, he and the Penguins would never again play for the Cup.

Mario Lemieux (1965–   )

Mario Lemieux's 199-point season in 1988–1989 and his leadership in the Penguins' two Stanley Cup titles stand out among his greatest moments. But Lemieux will also be remembered for two off-ice achievements that are as important as what he did on the ice. In 1993, he was diagnosed with Hodgkin's Disease, which is a form of cancer. Two months later, Lemieux was back on the ice, having missed only 23 games. He later took a year off to recover fully. In that time he founded the Mario Lemieux Foundation, which raises money for cancer research. He also saved the Penguins for the city of Pittsburgh. In 1998, the team went bankrupt and was at risk of moving or folding. The team owed Lemieux more money than it did anyone else, so Lemieux put together an ownership group and bought the team. When he made his comeback in 2000, Lemieux did it as a player and an owner.

1993–1994 New York Rangers

The New York Rangers were one of hockey's "Original Six." Their last Stanley Cup win came in 1940. Each year, the team was taunted in every rink with chants of "1940." In 1993, the Rangers turned to a fiery coach named Mike Keenan. He had taken two teams to the Stanley Cup finals, but players didn't like his harsh methods. The Rangers had talent, but they didn't work very hard as a team. Keenan changed that. He was known for getting his players in shape.

The Rangers didn't even make the playoffs in 1992–1993, but Keenan came in and told his players that his goal for them was to win the Stanley Cup. The players believed that they could do it. Keenan hung a picture of the Stanley Cup in their locker room so that the players would be reminded what they were playing for.

Rangers captain Mark Messier skates during a game against the New Jersey Devils.

Mike Keenan (1949–   )

Mike Keenan's tough rules brought the best out of his players. He went to the Stanley Cup finals three times with the Blackhawks and Flyers, but both times he left when he couldn't get along with his bosses. He was in New York less than a month in the fall of 1993 when he smashed a stick on the goal during practice. The Rangers got the message, and went on to finish first overall and win the Cup. During the summer, Keenan argued with general manager Neil Smith and jumped to the St. Louis Blues to take on the dual roles of general manager and coach.

The Rangers had three great players. Mark Messier was the captain and leader. The Rangers had gotten Messier from the Edmonton Oilers, as well as Adam Graves. Messier had won championships in Edmonton, and his teammates listened to him and respected him, knowing that he could help them win a championship. Brian Leetch was one of the game's best young defensemen, as was rookie Sergei Zubov. The Rangers also had a young goalie named Mike Richter who was ready to become a star. Richter had spent time in the minor leagues the previous year, but he showed he could play at the professional level. He won a league-high 42 games during the regular season!

The Rangers started out the season 4–5. They were very frustrated and coach Keenan was very angry and disappointed with his team. Keenan motivated his team and they won twelve out of their next fourteen games. They moved into first place and never looked back. They were in first place the rest of the season.

In the first round of the playoffs the Rangers swept their rivals, the Islanders, outscoring them 22–3. In the second round, they faced the Washington Capitals, beating them four games to one.

In the **conference** finals, the Rangers met their rivals from across the Hudson River, the New Jersey Devils. The Devils hadn't beaten the Rangers in six regular season games, but it wasn't the regular season anymore. It was a great series full of big goals and big saves. The series had three double overtime games! The Devils led the series after Game 5, but Messier had something to say. Before Game 6, he guaranteed the Rangers would win. He made sure they did—by scoring a hat trick! The Rangers won Game 7 in double overtime and advanced to the Cup finals.

HISTORY BOX

Lockout!

In April 1992, NHL players staged a brief 30-game strike to protest working conditions. That dispute was solved in time for the playoffs. Three years later, when the agreement expired, NHL owners shut down the league in the fall of 1994 when a new deal couldn't be reached. The season's start was delayed until January, as players wanted more freedom of movement and owners wanted to put a stop to huge rises in salaries. The 105-day lockout couldn't have come at a worse time for the NHL. The Rangers' win captured the attention of both New York and the nation, and hockey was labeled a "hot" sport. The lockout didn't solve much—a decade later, in 2004, the owners once again locked out the players.

In the finals, the Vancouver Canucks gave the Rangers everything they could handle. The Rangers started out the series playing great, winning three games and losing only one. The Canucks came back and won Game 5 with a score of 6–3. The Rangers had a chance to win the series in Game 6, but Vancouver won at home 4–1 to send the series back to Madison Square Garden for Game 7. Messier scored to give the Rangers a 3–1 lead, but Vancouver scored in the third period to get within a goal. The Canucks attacked and attacked, but the Rangers held on for their first Stanley Cup in 54 years. In 2004, *The Hockey News* voted it the best Cup final of all time.

Mark Messier of the New York Rangers looks for the puck in a game against the Montreal Candiens.

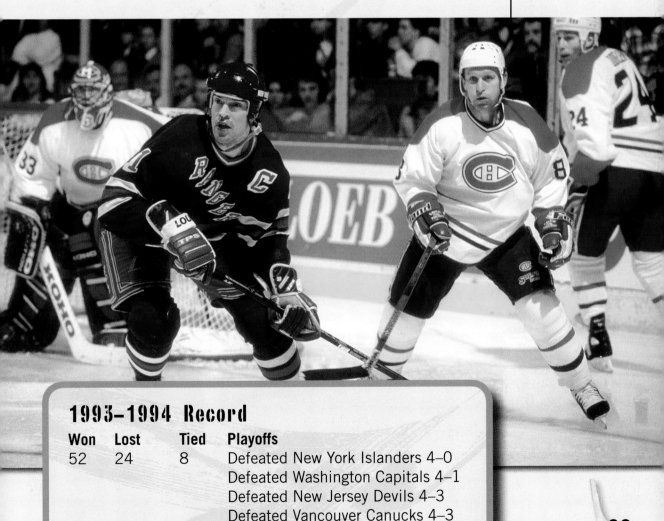

1993–1994 Record

Won	Lost	Tied	Playoffs
52	24	8	Defeated New York Islanders 4–0
			Defeated Washington Capitals 4–1
			Defeated New Jersey Devils 4–3
			Defeated Vancouver Canucks 4–3

After moving to Denver from Quebec City in 1995, the Avalanche quickly became one of the NHL's most successful **franchises**. Joe Sakic and Peter Forsberg, two of the game's best forwards, were already on board as well as the game's best goalie, Patrick Roy.

The Avalanche won their second Stanley Cup in 2001, but it was the first for Ray Bourque. One of the best defensemen of his generation, Bourque had spent all twenty seasons of his career in Boston. After two unsuccessful trips to the finals with the Bruins, Bourque wanted another chance to win the Cup before his career ended. He asked for a trade to Colorado in 2000.

A promising 1999-2000 team became a great one in 2000-2001 when Ray Bourque joined.

The Dead-Puck Era

The Colorado Avalanche was one of the few teams in the league with plenty of offensive talent. At this time, most teams were concentrating on defense and making it almost impossible for other teams to score. When the Devils won the Cup in 1995, they did it with a system known as the "neutral-zone trap," which puts lots of players in the middle of the ice and reduces offensive chances. By 2000, nearly every team in the league was using a method of the trap. In 1983–1984, the Oilers scored 446 goals. In 2002–2003, no team scored more than 269, and 2 teams scored fewer than 2 goals per game.

The Avalanche had the best regular season record of 52–16–10–4 (Wins–Losses–Ties–Overtime Losses). Patrick Roy made history as he broke Terry Sawchuck's record for career wins with 448. After avoiding Detroit and Dallas in the playoffs, the Avalanche faced the Devils in the finals. Bourque and Colorado could not be stopped. Bourque's motto was "16W"—the number of wins needed to win the Cup, and the exit off the New Jersey Turnpike that led to the Meadowlands, where the Devils played.

In Game 1, the Avalanche came out strong behind two goals from star Joe Sakic and one each from Rob Blake, Chris Drury, and Steven Reinprecht. The Avalanche won easily, 5–0, shutting out the Devils. Patrick Roy was great in the win, stopping all 26 shots he faced. It was his third playoff shutout, and eighteenth of the year, as he extended his Stanley Cup winning streak to nine games.

New Jersey came back in Game 2. Colorado's Joe Sakic scored the first goal of the game with only six minutes played, but his team would not score again. The Devils came back in the first period. Neither of the teams scored again, but that was enough to lead New Jersey to a 2–1 victory, as they tied the series up at 1–1.

The Avalanche started out Game 3 losing 1–0, but Martin Skoula, Ray Bourque, and Dan Hinote all scored goals, giving their team a 3–1 victory and a 2–1 series lead. However, New Jersey wasn't about to lose two games in a row. They out shot the Avalanche 35–12 in Game 4, and ended up with a 3–2 victory. The series was tied 2–2.

Game 5 went to New Jersey, who won 4–1. This loss was Colorado's worst loss of the post-season. Until this game, they had not trailed in the playoffs by more than one goal. It was also the first time they lost back-to-back playoff games. Instead of feeling sorry for themselves, they came out strong in Game 6. Roy recorded his second shutout of the series, and fourth of the playoffs as Colorado won 4–0. Roy blocked all 24 shots that came at him, including 12 in the first period. Adam Foote, Ville Nieminen, Chris Drury, and Alex Tanguay all scored goals for the Avalanche, tying the series at 3–3. This forced a seventh game at their home arena.

Patrick Roy (1965–   )

Patrick Roy retired in 2003 with a claim to the title of hockey's greatest goaltender ever. He won the Stanley Cup with Montreal as a rookie in 1986, and led the Canadiens to glory again in 1993. But in December 1995, Montreal coach Mario Tremblay refused to take him out of the net on a night when the Canadiens lost 11–1. When he was finally replaced, Roy said he would never play for Montreal again. Traded to Colorado, he led the Avalanche to the Stanley Cup that season and another in 2001. He is the NHL's all-time leader in games played by a goalie (1,029), wins (551), and playoff wins (151).

The Avalanche score against the New Jersey Devils in Game 1 of the Stanley Cup Finals.

2000–2001 Record

Won	Lost	Tied	OTL	Playoffs
52	16	10	4	Defeated Vancouver Canucks 4–0
				Defeated Los Angeles Kings 4–3
				Defeated St. Louis Blues 4–1
				Defeated New Jersey Devils 4–3

OTL=Overtime Losses

No one in the history of the NHL waited as long as Bourque to win the Stanley Cup, and he finally got it in Game 7. Star Joe Sakic scored a goal and assisted on one in the game, bringing his total to thirteen goals and thirteen assists for the playoffs. Alex Tanguay was the star of the game, scoring 2 goals to lead the Avalanche to a 3–1 victory, and their second Stanley Cup in 5 years. Goalie Roy had 25 stops and because of his excellent play in the playoffs was awarded the Conn Smythe Trophy.

After the victory, NHL Commissioner Gary Bettman handed the Cup to Avalanche captain Sakic to hoist above his head. But instead of lifting the Cup, Sakic passed it to Bourque. After 22 seasons in the NHL, Bourque capped his Hall of Fame career by raising the Cup above his head.

The Final Score

It is almost impossible to narrow hockey's great teams down to just ten. So many great teams and great players have been left out. But that is part of the fun of hockey, because there have been so many greats. What makes a great team is how long they have lived on in the memories of those who have seen them play. There is a Stanley Cup winner every single year, but it is the teams that capture the hearts and minds of the fans and public who earn their place among the greatest.

This book has named many great teams, from the greatest of all time. From the 1976–1977 Montreal Canadiens, who won an amazing 60 games during the season and only lost 8 times, to the highest scoring and best offensive team of all time, the 1983–1984 Edmonton Oilers. The Oilers had hockey's greatest player of all time, Wayne Gretzky. A great team can also be determined by an unstoppable goalie, such as Colorado in 2000–2001. Goalie Patrick Roy, who still has the most wins in hockey history, led the team to a championship. Coaches can also lead a team to greatness, as Mike Keenan did for the 1993–1994 New York Rangers. The Rangers didn't even make the playoffs the year before, but Keenan taught them to play hard and believe in themselves, and they ended up winning the Stanley Cup.

Every spring, a new argument begins. Is this year's Stanley Cup champion one of the best of all time? That debate lasts until the new season begins. Each time the Stanley Cup is lifted by a winning player, fans argue whether the new champion should be added to the list of true greats. Maybe someday your favorite team will win a Stanley Cup, and be remembered as one of the greatest teams of all time!

The 1996–1997 Detroit Red Wings pose for a picture after winning the Stanley Cup.

Stanley Cup Winners 1960–2004

1960–1961 Chicago Blackhawks
1961–1962 Toronto Maple Leafs
1962–1963 Toronto Maple Leafs
1963–1964 Toronto Maple Leafs
1964–1965 Montreal Canadiens
1965–1966 Montreal Canadiens
1966–1967 Toronto Maple Leafs
1967–1968 Montreal Canadiens
1968–1969 Montreal Canadiens
1969–1970 Boston Bruins
1970–1971 Montreal Canadiens
1971–1972 Boston Bruins
1972–1973 Montreal Canadiens
1973–1974 Philadelphia Flyers
1974–1975 Philadelphia Flyers
1975–1976 Montreal Canadiens
1976–1977 Montreal Canadiens
1977–1978 Montreal Canadiens
1978–1979 Montreal Canadiens
1979–1980 New York Islanders
1980–1981 New York Islanders
1981–1982 New York Islanders
1982–1983 New York Islanders
1983–1984 Edmonton Oilers
1984–1985 Edmonton Oilers
1985–1986 Montreal Canadiens
1986–1987 Edmonton Oilers
1987–1988 Edmonton Oilers
1988–1989 Calgary Flames
1989–1990 Edmonton Oilers

Martin St. Louis scores his backhand against Calgary Flames in 2004.

1990–1991 Pittsburgh Penguins
1991–1992 Pittsburgh Penguins
1992–1993 Montreal Canadiens
1993–1994 New York Rangers
1994–1995 New Jersey Devils
1995–1996 Colorado Avalanche
1996–1997 Detroit Red Wings
1997–1998 Detroit Red Wings
1998–1999 Dallas Stars
1999–2000 New Jersey Devils
2000–2001 Colorado Avalanche
2001–2002 Detroit Red Wings
2002–2003 New Jersey Devils
2003–2004 Tampa Bay Lightning

Glossary

Art Ross Trophy award given to the player that finishes the season with the most points

assist passes that lead to a goal; as many as two assists can be awarded on one goal

body check when a player uses a hip or shoulder to bump an opponent off the puck

conference in hockey, teams are grouped into two conferences—the Eastern Conference and the Western Conference

Conn Smythe Trophy award given to the MVP for his team in the playoffs

decade period of ten years

dominate control something

dynasty in sports, a team that maintains its great position for a long time

face-off dropping the puck between two players to restart play

forward line three forwards—a left wing, center, and right wing—who enter and leave the ice as a group

franchise professional sports team organization. For example, Tampa Bay Lightning is a franchise.

hat trick three goals in one game

Hockey Hall of Fame organization that honors the best hockey players and coaches throughout history

momentum driving force

Most Valuable Player (MVP) hockey award given to the player who helps his team the most. The actual award is called the Hart Trophy.

National Hockey League (NHL) professional hockey league that was founded in 1917. As of 2004, there were 30 teams in the NHL.

overtime extra time added to a game when the teams are tied

period a hockey game is divided into 3, 20-minute periods

pioneer person who is the first to do something new

power play when a player serves a penalty, the opposing team has a one-man advantage, usually for two minutes or until the team on the power play scores

shutout game in which one team fails to score a goal

Stanley Cup silver trophy awarded to the NHL champions

sweep winning all of the games in a series

veteran older, more experienced player

Vezina Trophy hockey award given to the league's best goalie

World Hockey Association (WHA) professional hockey league that was created in 1972 to compete with the NHL. The WHA merged with the NHL in the 1979–1980 season.

Further Information

Further reading

Schnaber, Dean. *Sergei Federov*. Langhorne, PA: Chelsea House Publishers, 1999

Stewart, Mark Alan. *Mario Lemieux*: *Own the Ice*. Minneapolis: Twenty-First Century Books, Inc., 2004

Targ Brill, Marlene. *Ice Hockey*. Lake Forest, IL: Forest House Publishing Company, Inc., 2001

Walker, Niki, and Sarah Dann. *Hockey in Action*. New York: Crabtree Publishing Company, 1999

Addresses

Hockey Hall of Fame
BCE Place
30 Yonge Street
Toronto Ontario
Canada M5E 1X8
www.hhof.com

International Hockey Hall of Fame
277 York Street
Kingston, ON K7L 4V6
Canada
www.ihhof.com

The National Hockey League (NHL)
www.nhl.com

Index

Anderson, Glenn 28, 30

Armstrong, George 14, 15

Art Ross Trophy 10

Beliveau, Jean 10, 11, 12, 13, 15

Bossy, Mike 24, 26, 27

Boston Bruins 16–19, 21, 22, 23, 33, 40

Bourque, Ray 40, 41, 42, 43

Bower, Johnny 14, 15

Bowman, Scotty 20, 21, 32

Calgary Flames 29

Cheevers, Gerry 17, 22

Chicago Blackhawks 14, 33, 34, 37

Colorado Avalanche 40–43, 44

Conn Smythe Trophy 21, 23, 27, 34, 43

Delvecchio, Alex 6, 7, 8

Detroit Red Wings 6-9, 10, 12

Detroit Vipers 9

Drury, Chris 41, 42

Dryden, Ken 20, 21, 22

dynasties 4

Edmonton Oilers 28–31, 37, 41, 44

Esposito, Phil 16, 19

Francis, Ron 32, 34

Fuhr, Grant 28, 29, 30

Geoffrion, Bernie 8, 10, 12, 13

Gillies, Clark 24, 27, 30

Gretzky, Wayne 4, 9, 28, 30, 31, 33, 44

Hart Trophy 18

Hockey Hall of Fame 10, 20, 29

Howe, Gordie 4, 6, 7, 8, 9, 12, 33

Jagr, Jaromir 32, 34

Keenan, Mike 36, 37, 38, 44

Kurri, Jari 28, 30

Lafleur, Guy 12, 20, 21, 23

Lemaire, Jacques 20, 23

Lemieux, Mario 4, 28, 32, 33, 34, 35

Lindsay, Ted 6, 7, 8, 12

lockout 38

Los Angeles Kings 28, 30, 31

Messier, Mark 28, 37, 38, 39

Montreal Canadiens 7, 8, 10–13, 14, 15, 20–23, 42, 44

Most Valuable Player (MVP) 9, 18, 21

National Hockey League (NHL) 4, 9, 17, 24, 38

neutral-zone trap 41

New Jersey Devils 38, 41, 42

New York Islanders 21, 24–27, 28, 30, 38

New York Rangers 12, 24, 26, 33, 36–39, 44

Norris Trophy 18

Orr, Bobby 4, 16, 17, 18, 19

Pittsburgh Penguins 25, 32–35

Plante, Jacques 10, 11

power play 11

Pulford, Bob 14, 15

Richard, Maurice 10, 11, 12, 33

Roy, Patrick 40, 41, 42, 43, 44

safety gear 4

St. Louis Blues 17, 18, 19, 21, 37

Sakic, Joe 40, 41, 43

Sawchuck, Terry 14, 15, 41

Schutt, Steve 20, 21, 22

Smith, Billy 24, 30

Stanley Cup 5

Tanguay, Alex 42, 43

Toronto Maple Leafs 7, 14–15

Tremblay, Mario 22, 42

Vancouver Canucks 26, 27, 39

Vezina Trophy 11, 21

Washington Capitals 38

World Hockey Association (WHA) 9, 24